LIVING OUTSIDE THE BOX

Finding Normal in a World of Disabilities

LIVING OUTSIDE THE BOX

Finding Normal in a World of Disabilities

SHEILA SAXTON

TATE PUBLISHING
AND ENTERPRISES, LLC

Published by Tate Publishing & Enterprises, LLC
127 E. Trade Center Terrace | Mustang, Oklahoma 73064 USA
1.888.361.9473 | www.tatepublishing.com

Tate Publishing is committed to excellence in the publishing industry. The company reflects the philosophy established by the founders, based on Psalm 68:11,
"The Lord gave the word and great was the company of those who published it."

Book design copyright © 2015 by Tate Publishing, LLC. All rights reserved.
Cover design by Ivan Charlem Igot
Interior design by Manolito Bastasa

Published in the United States of America

ISBN: 978-1-63367-457-8
1. Family & Relationships / Parenting / Motherhood
2. Family & Relationships / Children with Special Needs
15.01.28

ACKNOWLEDGMENTS

First and foremost I want to thank my Lord and Savior Jesus for giving me this normal life that he has chosen just for me. I thank him for leading me through the good and bad times with his kindness and love. With out him, I am nothing.

I want to thank my children for being who they are. All of you are amazing, and I love you with all my heart.

I personally would never have thought of writing a book if were not for my dear friend, Heather who put the thought in my head and convinced me I have a story worth telling. She was the first person to review each chapter and encourage me to keep going. You are a true and faithful friend.

CONTENTS

THE MAKING
OF A NORMAL LIFE

Few of us start our journey into adulthood knowing what our mission is going to be. We have ideas and dreams of what life will be. But that life often takes us on a journey that we never expected. Sometimes, the exact opposite of what we expected. Once we have traveled part way down the road of life, we can look back and see Gods hand leading us in the direction He intended from the beginning. We can see times that we missed the signs we were meant to see and veered off that chosen path. But other times, it can be very comforting when you see that you are finally catching on to Gods will and beginning to live the life he had in store for you all along. Then the trick is, to find normal in the life he has given you.

Where I Came From

I grew up in small town America in a time that we ran the neighborhood with friends and came home at mealtime and when the sun went down. I had a perfectly wonderful childhood with loving parents and terrific grandparents. We were not a monetarily rich family, but I never knew that. We had everything we needed and more. My mother made every Holiday a celebration—from heart-shaped cakes on Valentines Day to window silhouettes of Presidents Washington and Lincoln for their birthdays. We were the house all the other kids came to.

I didn't grow up knowing much about disabilities, mostly because I was afraid to ask. My grandmother had brothers with severe disabilities, but they were old men to me, and very scary. They made noises that I could not understand, some of them walked in a jerking motion and flung their arms wildly as they walked. Mostly they just sat in chairs or stayed in their bedrooms. I remember Great-Grandpa carried plates of food to one of them and saying, "I'm going to feed my baby!" and he would smile the biggest smile as he disappeared into the back room. He looked as if it was a great joy to go back there. All I could see in that room was a bed with a tall wooden side and occasionally an arm would wave above the wood panel. There was another brother that Great-Grandma would tell us to watch out for, because "he falls a lot." He seemed like a very tall man to me. I was always worried he would fall, and I did not want to see that happen. I would try to fall asleep in the car going from Grandmother's house across town to my great-grandparents' house. That way, I could just stay in the car and not have to go in the house. I loved my great-grandparents very much, but I was just so afraid of "the boys" as they called them. These men all went to be with Jesus when I was still very young. I don't know why I never ask questions about them, I was just scared of them. Looking back now, I know it was just their life, it was their normal, and no one ever thought of explaining to a little girl what it meant to take care of a person with a disability, or that a disability is not the same thing as being sick. Now I wish I asked. I think I would have liked to sit beside that bed and get to know the man attached to the waving arm.

All of my childhood, I was horrified of sickness. In my mind having a disability was the same as being sick, I think. I don't know why these thoughts were always in my head. I was always worried about being sick. I would run from anyone that seemed to be sick. If a classmate got sick, I would worry myself into sickness and have to go home. I was scared when anyone in my family was sick. Going to the doctor was horrifying to me. I hated sitting in the waiting room. All those sick people, what if something happened right before my eyes, who would help them? What if I caught what they had on top of what I already had? What if the doctor couldn't help me, and I would stay sick forever? Being sick takes you out of control of your own body—that was horrifying to me. I needed to have control. I was always a worrier. I would feel sheer panic about these things. While I lived on the edge of panic, I was very determined never to let that show. I was seen as the tough one to most people outside my immediate family. No one ever thought anything fazed me. I appeared to be able to handle anything.

I remember when I was in junior high and my dad was in the hospital. I was horrified to go and visit him. I did not want to see him like that. He was strong. I could seldom remember him being sick. My mother had to almost force me to go see him.

When I was sixteen, I was invited to a revival at a church. That night, I saw peace in those people that I knew I needed. I had never felt peace in my heart before. That night I met Jesus for myself. I prayed and ask him to come into my heart and be my Savior. Finding Jesus gave me peace. I was still the tough-on-the-outside, weak-on-the-inside person. That's just who I am. But, a lot of the panic-type fears were much less. I had a hope, and someone that was always there to listen to my most inner thoughts and fears. With Jesus in my life, I didn't have to be in control of everything anymore.

Being Instantly Thrust into the World of Disabilities

As I was expecting my third child, my life was about to change in ways I would have never thought I could handle. In one day, my husband told me he wanted a divorce, and I told him I was pregnant. I begged him to stay until the baby was born, and he agreed to do that.

About half way through the pregnancy, I ate contaminated ice cream. It was just plain store-bought vanilla ice cream we had one evening. The next day, all the local TV channels were broadcasting warnings about this brand of ice cream and said to look on the end of the carton for a series of numbers. If your carton had the numbers be sure and watch the evening news to get the full story. I checked my freezer and sure enough, mine had the matching numbers. I tuned into the news that night to find out it was only dangerous if you were pregnant. The contaminant was causing miscarriage, premature delivery, or stillborn births. Obviously, I panicked. I got a hold of my doctor the next morning, and he prescribed high-powered antibiotics. I questioned the safety of the drug to the baby and was informed the risk of the drug was not near as serious as not taking it could be.

A few weeks later, when I was having my routine sonogram, it quickly became apparent that things were not normal. The nurse kept looking and re-looking, getting less and less talkative. Then she left the room and came back with the doctor. Never a good sign. He continued to look and measure the baby. Finally, he began explaining that the baby's legs were not measuring right, they were much too short. Through the next few appointments, he really didn't mention it again. So I was thinking it wasn't going to be that big of a deal. My baby was going to have short legs; his dad had short legs for his height, so it would be fine.

Shortly before the delivery, the doctor asked me if I was prepared for a child with Dwarfism or some similar disability. I'm sure he thought he had explained his suspicions to me, but he had not. I was devastated. I had no idea what I would do with a child with disabilities. I did inquire if the ice cream could be the reason something was wrong. The doctor said we would have to wait until delivery to be sure, and since I was the only pregnancy that had sustained through the contaminant, he didn't know; however, he was leaning more toward a genetic condition.

When my son was born, he was not breathing due to a cord complication. His legs were very short, hips were not formed right, and the bones on the back of his head were not fully formed. His head felt much like a water balloon. He was immediately shipped off to a nearby children's hospital. Our hospital tried to have the helicopter come and get my baby, but we were in tornado warnings that night, so he had to go by ambulance. I didn't even get to hold him; we barely got him named before he was on his way. The next time I saw Tyler, two days later, he had oxygen and a nasal g-tube taped to his face. He just lay perfectly still in the NICU (Neonatal Intensive Care Unit). His breathing was erratic and his legs lay abnormally to the sides. I was told he had a broken leg. I was horrified. What was our life going to be like now? This was *not* a *normal* baby. I loved him dearly but felt so inadequate to care for him. I just sat there in the NICU and cried, staring straight at him, telling him how much I loved him. I couldn't look at the other babies in the unit. So many sick babies with so many tubes coming out of them and machines beeping.

The children's hospital was about an hour away, so we visited him every day and went home to my girls at night. On about the third day, we were taken into a consultation room. The doctor said they were still running tests but confirmed it was a genetic disease, possibly osteogenesis imperfecta. This was the same disease our local hospital had suspected after delivery. We went through a lot of ups and downs over that week. No one was telling us anything. One very kind nurse took us aside and told us she didn't like the way the doctors would not tell the parents anything until all the tests were final. She explained they had ruled out that condition days ago and were looking at other genetic diseases. She said it was not her place to tell us anything, and she could get it a lot of trouble if anyone found out; however, the prognosis we had been given was terrible, and she wanted us to know that was not necessarily what we were looking at. That sweet woman did ease my fears. Finally on the sixth day, Tyler was diagnosed with hypophosphatasia, a rare genetic bone disease. His body was missing the enzyme that transfers phosphorus from the blood to the bones. There was no treatment; it's genetic. All long bones were extremely weak, especially his legs. The prognosis was different but still not good. He would never reach five feet tall and fractures would be a huge concern his entire life. Only time would tell how easily his bones would break.

At that moment, I was thrown into the world of disease, disabilities, doctors, nurses, sick children, and hopelessness everywhere. I was in control of nothing. All the fears of my childhood were being thrown back in my face. I had a choice to make. I could either return to those fears of my childhood, or I could walk in faith that my Jesus had me here for a reason. He would never leave me or forsake me. I chose the latter. It was not easy; we had to find a new normal for our family.

We went home and explained to my two and four-year-old daughters what was going on with their baby brother. My four-year-old listened intently. A few minutes later, she returned and said, "Jesus just told me, my baby brother's leg is healed." When we returned to the hospital the next day, we were surprised to find out they did nothing to treat Tyler's broken leg. We had been told they would cast the leg that evening after we left. I ask the nurse why it hadn't been cast yet. She explained that when they redid the x-ray, it showed the leg had healed a lot more than they originally thought, so it would just be splinted before we took him home the next day. We were thrilled!

That night I explained to the girls that his leg was almost completely healed. I told them we needed to thank Jesus for that. My precious little four-year-old prayer warrior looked me straight in the eyes and said, "No! Jesus told me he healed his leg. It's healed." I did not want to belittle her faith, so I tried to explain that it was a miracle that it had healed so much. She was insistent. We went back the next morning so excited to bring our baby home, only to find out his leg had not been splinted. I was so upset, expecting this would delay his discharge while we waited. The nurse came in and said he was ready to go home. When they took him to splint the leg, they x-rayed one last time and confirmed that the fracture was healed. When we got home and told his sister, she just smiled at me with those beautiful big brown eyes and said, "I told you. Jesus said he healed his leg." Never underestimate the power of a child's faith.

By the time my son turned three years old, he had suffered six broken legs. We spent a large part of our lives at the nearby children's hospital. So much in fact, Tyler called the hospital cafeteria "my restaurant" and would ask to go there for lunch when we weren't even in the city. God was faithful to me. I quickly understood that disability did not mean sick. My son was not sick—he was very healthy—he just had a genetic bone disease. My Lord not only eased my fears, he actually brought me to the point I could sit and converse with other parents in the waiting rooms. We would discuss what conditions our children had, and what all they had gone through. I was finding a new normal around all the chaos and stress.

When my children look back on those years, they don't talk about feeling hopeless or about sickness or disability. They talk about the boat at the hospital; it was in one of the waiting rooms. They could walk in it and pretend they were in a real boat. They remember the ramp on the way to the genetics clinic and how we would let the stroller go really fast down it. They remember always going to the big toy store on our way home from the hospital and eating at a fancy restaurant. They say they understand now how stressful that time must have been for me. But they agreed they never felt the stress. It was just normal life for them.

As for the marriage, we fought to hold it together for a few years. I remember reading, 90 percent of marriages end in divorce after the birth of a disabled child or the death of a child. That's very sad. At a time when the parents need each other so much, it becomes impossible to fight for the child's needs and for the marriage. However, for us, we were just prolonging the inevitable and ended in divorce.

Choosing to Step into the World of Disabilities with Another Child

There are posters with beautiful little babies' faces and the words *never, never, never shake a baby*. We've all seen them. We shudder a little at the thought of a child being hurt. While that is a very important message that needs to be gotten out.…Have you ever thought about what life is like for the precious children that survive the abuse?

I had been a foster parent since before my first child was born. I became a foster parent to give a home to babies that were awaiting adoption. It was my small stand against abortion. I wanted to help give a safe home for some special little ones as their forever families got ready for them. After a few years though, very few babies were being given up for adoption in our area. So I started taking children that were under school age.

My fourth child, my son, was born a perfectly normal, wonderful baby. Between the ages of three and four months, he endured repeated severe abuse at the hands of his birth family. The records describe his last abusive incident as being beat head to toe, forcefully shaken, and thrown against a wall. He had a concussion, broken ribs, a broken leg, and bruises over most of his small body. He suffered significant damage in all four lobes of his brain. When he came to us as a foster child, he was deemed an "unadoptable" child. He came to join our family at twenty months old. Wesley was my son from the first moment I looked into those beautiful blue eyes, and he reached up and rubbed my face.

He is now seventeen years old. He is the joy of my life, and to his brother and three sisters. He is cortically blind, which means his eyes are fully functioning but because of the severity of brain damage, his brain does not know the eyes work. He has a seizure disorder. He is unable to speak because his speech center was destroyed in the abuse. He has a severe sensory processing disorder. The sensory issues make him appear profoundly autistic. However, he does not lack understanding of spoken language as many children with autism do. He knows quite well what is being said and also knows what he wants to say.

Our normal has forever changed with the addition of a multiply disabled child.

Searching for a Child with a Disability

I had friends that were in the process of adopting a little girl from China. We talked about the adoption process often since adoption was a part of both of our families. Then one day, my friend came to me and said she had seen a post on an adoption message board about a little deaf girl in China. All of the fees for the adoption agency were being waived or somehow paid because she was a disabled child. My friend really felt like I needed to check it out. By the time I found the child, she had already found her forever family. That started my search for my deaf daughter. I was sure she was out there. I searched adoption websites from all over the world the most promising seemed like China or Guatemala. Through a series of seeming coincidences, I did find her, and she was only about an hour away from me. When I retraced the time frame of searching for her, I started looking for her when she was three months old.

My precious fifth child came to us right before her fourth birthday. The first time I met her, she crawled up on my lap and fell asleep. Her caseworker said she had never seen her attach to anyone like that. I told her it was because she *is* my daughter. She has a severe hearing loss in both ears, ADHD, asthma, and more food allergies than most people can fathom.

Avalon is now fifteen years old. She is all too quickly, to me, becoming a beautiful young woman. She attends our state school for the deaf. She is on student council, plays basketball, volleyball, runs track, and is a cheerleader. She loves horses, swimming, and talking to her friends on her video phone.

Her normal is different than all the rest of our family since she lives at her school during the week and comes home to us on weekends, holidays, and for the summer.

Facing Your Own Immortality

I had never considered that I might be faced with a serious illness or disability. I am the care giver. I take care of all my children's needs. Then one day, after some tests, my doctor called me herself. I must admit, fear instantly set in when the conversation started with her saying she felt she needed to call me personally with the results. She said the biopsy came back positive. I had malignant melanoma. I had known I had the spots for over a year and had ignored it. I was too afraid to face what might happen. Now it was reality. I put a smile on my face to hide the fear and told everyone I was fine. I had a friend that had been through this; he and his wife were probably the only ones that truly knew what I was going through. Their support and understanding was invaluable. They let me talk about my fears, they understood the tears, and they sat beside me at the doctor's office to help understand my treatment options. I worried about what would happen to my youngest two children if I couldn't take care of them. Their day-to-day needs were all consuming. No one really knew what it was like to care for them. We didn't lead what most people would consider a normal life in any way. I didn't talk about those struggles because first of all I didn't want pity. And second and more importantly, I want the world to see my children for the incredible people they are, not for their disabilities. I had another dear friend that came to stay with me when I had surgery. She was also the mother of a child with disabilities and knew what it took to care for my little ones.

I was very blessed. I had five spots that needed biopsies, only one was cancerous. After it was removed, the cancer was only surface deep. Aside from an eight-inch scar down my back, I was fine, no further treatment needed. We are all a little more careful about wearing sunscreen. I have regular check ups every six months to make sure it hasn't reoccurred. Melanoma is a very unpredictable cancer; it can reoccur at any time and is never considered to be in remission.

Life went very quickly back to our normal.

Accepting My Own Disability

What happens when the care giver needs help? My normal has now been forever changed as I am forced to accept the fact that I now have a life-changing disability.

Three years ago, I started down this road. I began having a lot of trouble being dizzy. It was a very different kind of dizzy than I had ever had before, and it would last several days or even weeks at a time. My first blood work showed severe vitamin D deficiency. This is fairly common with melanoma survivors, because we should stay out of the sun completely. That was corrected with a vitamin supplement, but the dizziness remained. I had always fought anemia. The next possibility was that menopause was being very unkind to me. Although blood work only showed borderline anemia, maybe that was the cause. So, I altered my diet to make sure I was getting ample iron. The doctor increased my iron supplement, but the dizziness persisted. Then we went through the possibility of chronic ear infections being the cause. That had been an issue since childhood. After treating that, the dizziness was still getting worse, not better. It had been an entire year, and I had only had three weeks that I had not been dizzy. So next, I was referred to an allergist because of the ear issues. He tested and found no allergies, which was quite a surprise to me. I had been told by doctors my whole life that I had seasonal and environmental allergies that were causing ear problems. This allergist diagnosed reflux that was causing the constant fluid in my ears. He treated that, and over all I did feel better. My ears were not having any of the troubles I had always battled. However, the dizziness was no better. It was now constant and affecting every area of my life. He sent me on to an ear specialist. More tests. The ears specialist found nothing wrong and sent me to a balance center. On the initial intake, the receptionist told me, at the end of their testing, I would have a diagnosis and a treatment plan. She assured me answers, I was so relieved. At this point, I had been forced to take medical leave from work. Mostly due to the fact that I was too dizzy to drive. At the end of the three-hour testing, I was expecting answers. Unfortunately, the doctors kept using phrases like, "I'm not sure, I've never seen this before, how can that be." They explained a few things to me. Basically my vestibular system seemed to be burned out. One of the things the doctors found puzzling was that I should not be able to walk or stand at all with that much damage. They explained that the only way I was still walking was by "sheer will." Maybe that strong will to be in control did have a purpose for me. Not my will but thine came to my mind, it was only by the grace of God that I could even function. They ended my session by ordering an MRI. When that came back fine, it confirmed what they thought about my vestibular system. I have bilateral vestibulopathy. They explained to me they had never seen a person with both sides burned out. Usually one side or the other is gone. In those cases, physical therapy teaches the good side to take over for what is gone. In my case, we would be trying to teach the brain to take over the balance function. The doctor told me later they really had no idea if it would work or not.

This condition is a side effect caused by certain antibiotics, a lot of which I was given for ear infections that I now knew were not ear infections in the first place but reflux.

I am still learning what normal is for me now.

Where We Are Now

I am a twice divorced mother of five wonderful children and grandmother to three terrific little ones. Children are my life. They always have been. In grade school, my best friend and I set up her garage with all our dolls as our orphanage. We played there for an entire summer, taking care of all our babies every day. I started babysitting when I was in junior high. I taught Bible school every summer from my teens until Tyler was born. All I ever wanted to be was a Mom. I loved the baby stage. I could sit and rock a baby for hours. The toddlers were a joy, watching them learn was fascinating. I was sad when my children started school. I didn't want to turn them over to anyone else. I counted the days until holidays and summer breaks.

I am still the tough one. I don't want to need help. I like to be in control. I will try and figure out how to take care of whatever happens to us. I do have great faith in Almighty God, and he has seen my children and me through many struggles. Those struggles would probably be easier if I gave up the control a lot sooner and let God work his wonders. His normal is so much better than anything I can imagine.

A Closer Look

A large part of living with disabilities is what you make of it. Every disability has its own challenges. They're all different. I do not pretend to understand what normal means to anyone else. I am not a professional anything; I don't have a degree in disabilities or education. I'm just a mom with a disability, raising kids with disabilities. I only want to share a little bit of what it is like to live with the few disabilities we know in our family. If you can start to understand what day-to-day life is like for a family dealing with disabilities, then I have been successful in spreading a tiny light of awareness and just maybe making life seem a little more normal for families like mine who live in very abnormal situations.

WHAT NORMAL LOOKS LIKE WITH AN INFANT WITH A CHRONIC DISEASE

Life with a chronic disease can be anything but normal. Taking care of my son was so much different than it had been with my baby girls. The carefree aspect of mothering a new baby was gone. His legs could break just turning over in bed. When he wore sleepers, I had to pin the legs together down the middle. The doctors had advised this because as an infant, if he flopped over in the night, it could break a leg. When he got old enough to roll over with control, we didn't have to do that any longer. The way I changed his diaper was different. You know the way you take a hold of a babies little feet and lift his bottom up to change the diaper? Lifting him with his feet could break his legs. We had to figure out how to lift his bottom without putting any stress on the legs and without allowing his legs to flop around unsupported. The way I patted him to sleep had to be done in a different way. A pat on his hips could break his leg. He couldn't be held by his sisters for more than a moment, they might jostle him wrong and that could break his legs. Leaving him with a sitter was not an option. I had to watch every movement he made to keep him safe. The usual baby furniture posed real dangers for Tyler. If I had him in a stroller out in public, I had to guard to make sure nothing bumped his legs. If we sat at the park for the girls to play, Tyler would sit in his stroller. I would have my leg completely over the stroller and across his legs to guard from anything bumping him. Tiny little legs hung out of the infant swings we had at that time. One bump as someone walked by would be all it took to send us back to the hospital with another broken leg. I had used front packs to carry my other babies, which would have put him in danger. Just putting him into a front pack could have broke him.

So Many Fractures

Each time Tyler broke a leg, it meant about a two-day stay at the children's hospital. He and I would stay at the hospital, his Dad would drive back and forth, and his sisters would stay with family friends. I often felt guilty for leaving my little girls so much even though it couldn't be helped. My friends were so good to take the girls at a moments notice, and they made their time with them seem like it was a special little vacation. It was just part of normal life to the girls. They knew every time their brother broke his leg they would go spend the night at a friend's house. They got very quick at grabbing what they needed for their special little visits. The girls could pack their bags and mine while I made the appropriate phone calls for someone to pick them up and got my son ready. One time in the emergency room, I remember looking down at my feet and seeing that my socks didn't match. I had just pulled on the socks the girls handed me and hadn't even looked at them.

One of his fractures was caused when his sister was playing with his tiny feet. She lifted his feet up just a small amount off the floor, when she let go and his feet bumped the ground it broke his leg. It was not forceful. She was not being too rough. He broke that easily.

When Tyler finally learned to crawl, it was so cute. Because of the disease, he was incredibly small. So he looked so tiny crawling across the floor. One evening we were at a friend's house, I put him on the floor to show off his crawling talents. He took off across her kitchen floor. At that same moment our four-year-olds were playing tug-of-war in the other room. One of them came flying through the doorway and fell over him. Not even on him, just stumbling over him. But it was enough of a bump as they stumbled over him to break his leg. The girls spent that night at that house with our friends as we headed back to the hospital.

As we visited with his doctor on one of his weekly check-ups for one of his broken legs, the doctor told us he would be leaving and would be moving to Chicago. The girls said, "Chicago, that's where Grandma lives!." The doctor asked if we visited them often. He then gave us what would be his number once he moved there. He said we might need him in Chicago. I thought that was so nice—it showed his love and commitment to the children he was treating. I stuck the number in my wallet.

My sweet little guy was getting so big, he learned to pull up and stand in front of the sofa. We were so excited; he was starting to cruise. One evening he did that while one of his sisters were sitting on the sofa. She picked up a small pillow and lightly bopped him on the top of his head. He started laughing and let go and fell to a sitting position. Broken leg. Again, this was not hard, or too rough. His legs just broke with normal activity. This incident happened as we were visiting my parents in Chicago. I pulled a note out of my wallet and called our old doctor. So we got to know another children's hospital, in another state, and consult the same doctor who was already a friend. This actually ended up being one of our best treatment plans. The doctor had us meet him in a treatment room, and we didn't even have to go through the emergency room—no waiting, no explaining a rare disease that emergency room staff have never heard of. Sometimes it's the small blessings that make it all bearable. The night we stayed in that hospital, we were in a ward with many other children. My sweet little boy kept crying out, "I go car now." He just wanted to go back to his grandparents house. One of the other moms came over to me and talked about what a sweet voice he had and how sad he sounded. She went on to tell me her son was six years old and had never spoken a word, saying he had autism. I had no idea what that was.

At one point, Tyler had just been out of a body cast for only two weeks. He flipped over while I was changing his diaper. I knew instantly his leg broke again. There was a certain cry that he only cried when he broke a leg. I never heard a cry like it any other time. By this time, I knew the sound all too well. I picked him up and looked at his leg. He also held them a certain way when they were broke, and he was doing that. There was no doubt. I was instantly overtaken with despair. He had just spent twelve weeks in a body cast, how was he ever going to get well if he continued to break his bones over and over again. The healing process in a cast always takes a toll on the bone strength; the lack of movement it takes to heal the fracture actually makes the bones weaker. It's not that drastic on normal bones. But his were already so weak. How was he ever going to regain any bone strength if he couldn't stay out of a cast? I was always very good at staying calm while I held him and got the girls to friend's houses. But when I started driving the hour to the hospital, the tears would start and I would just start praying. This night my prayer was, "God, I don't understand why. If his leg is still broken when we get to the hospital, then I am not stopping until you tell me why my baby has to go through this." It was a desperate prayer, not something I usually feel. Faith comes easy to me most of the time. As we approached the hospital, I pulled myself together. I lifted him carefully out of his car seat. I knew how to best handle him to minimize pain. Then I looked down at his leg, and he wasn't holding it in that distinct way he did when it was broken. I took him on in to the ER, and they x-rayed. It wasn't actually broke, just injured on the fracture line. All of the sudden the words of my prayer came back to me, "*If* it's still broken…I'm not giving up until you tell me why." God had answered me—the answer that I have never forgotten was that I don't need to know why. God knows why, and he is certainly better than I to be in control. I never again ask why we were going through this.

When my son was in his body casts, he didn't sleep much. With no physical activity, he required very little sleep and needed to be turned over every two hours to avoid bed sores inside the cast. A normal night's sleep for me has always been nine hours, that's what I have needed my whole life to function at my best. His time in casts ranged from six to twelve weeks, depending on the fracture. So I would become very low functioning by the end. Once I called a friend and she and her teenage daughter came and spent the night. They played with him, turned him, and just hung out one night so I could sleep. For a mom who loves being a mom and does not feel like it is an imposition on her own time in any way, and for a person who needs to be in control so badly, asking for this kind of help was one of the hardest things I had to do. Learning to ask for help does not come easy for me.

During one of our cast times, I remember being so physically exhausted house work completely stopped. A friend had stopped by to visit and was talking about how hard it was to keep up on house work since she had her third child. She explained that when she was single she vacuumed twice a day and now sometimes she only got it done every other day. I was sitting on the sofa barely able to move; my son was lying in the living room crib in a cast and our combined five other children were playing outside. I began to tell her what I had recently discovered.

"You know what I discovered? If you drop a bag of chips on the carpet and can't get them vacuumed up right away, they just disappear into the carpet."

I still remember her face. She was shocked and appalled but at my level of complete exhaustion, it seemed like a great revelation to me. I think she offered to vacuum for me, but I'm not sure if she did since I was so tired even the memory is foggy.

What Playtime Was Like

My little boy was a calm and gentle spirit from the beginning. God knew Tyler had to have that temperament for the life he was going to lead. He spent a large part of his first three years in spica hip casts. These casts go from his armpits to his toes. He had very limited mobility, although he did learn to roll over in some of them. He had a crib in the living room. He would lay in it like a king on his throne and watch all the normal activities of the day. To entertain him, we would color or play with some form of building blocks. He was so creative, loved to draw and build intricate creations. I had a developmental screening done on him when he was two years old. He was in a body cast at the time, so he scored at a 9 month old in gross motor skills, and at 4.5 years old in fine motor skills. His life was not normal to most people, children, or adults. He didn't get to play on playground equipment. When he went to birthday parties, he had to sit with his mom and watch the games. Many local restaurants have had play places with ball pits. My son would sit with me. Children would throw him a ball once in a while, and he would throw it back at them and laugh. It wasn't as sad as all that sounds—it was normal life for him—he didn't know any different. Kids at church knew at very young ages what they could do with Tyler and what they could not. While they were all young and had no real understanding, it really didn't matter, it was just normal for playing with him.

Facing the Terrible Twos

The terrible twos took on a whole new meaning with a child that could break a bone so easily. Most two-year-olds have no fear and are learning cause and effect by trial and error. They learn not to jump off tall furniture because it hurts, despite the fact that parents have warned them repeatedly. With my son, I had to watch every movement for any minor fall would break a leg. He could not be allowed to just climb around on toys or furniture. Every mom says she can't let the kids out of her sight; however, I literally could not let him out of my sight for a moment, and seldom out of my reach. He had to be lifted on and off a chair. I couldn't allow him to try climbing on it unless I had a hold him to keep him from slipping. If he came down off a chair a little too fast, the jarring when he hit the floor would break his leg. I also had a four and six-year-old to watch, so my normal was to do nothing but keep an eye on my children. I do realize that is every parents' job, but it was totally different too. I couldn't let the kids play in the living room while I cooked a meal. My son had to be in his highchair so I could see and protect him. I carried him with me if I needed to get the mail. He sat beside me in a stroller while I folded laundry. Every time I went into the bathroom, he had to be placed in a playpen to keep him from falling or keep the girls from bumping into him.

I had always planned on being a homeschooler. I did not think I could turn my babies over to strangers at such young ages. My oldest was hitting school age just as my son was full blown in the terrible twos. I would try to teach her while holding him on my hip. I couldn't put him down; he would crawl out of sight and possibly hurt himself. I managed to do kindergarten with her. But as first grade approached, I knew I could not adequately teach her and protect him. Our church had started its own school the year before, so I enrolled her for first grade. At least I was not turning her over to strangers I knew each teacher well. Not being able to homeschool my children was a disappointment to me, it was something I had always planned to do. But Tyler's safety and my sanity overruled, and plans were changed. Not a bad change necessarily, just not what I had expected.

Going Out in Public

It was hard enough to guard his every move at home, but taking him out in public was even more nerve-racking. It actually was easier to go out when he was in the body casts. At least then he was protected from minor bumps. When he was not in a cast, putting him in a shopping cart was a hazard. In order for him to sit in a cart and have his legs dangle loosely, my body could never move away from his legs. I had to be a constant block from anything bumping his legs. I could not take a step away to the side to grab something off a shelf. The girls learned to grab whatever I pointed at. I used it as a game when they were young: What can you reach? Who can get it first? Then it changed to a learning game: get the red can, get the can with the word *beans*. Whatever it took to keep him protected while we shopped, I did.

It's All a Matter of Perspective

Every time we went to a check up at the children's hospital, we had to start in a large waiting room to get our clinic card updated. This waiting room was also the waiting room for out patient chemotherapy. The first times we went, all I could do was look into my son's face; and the same phrase repeated over and over in my head. We are fine. His legs just break. My baby is not dying.

I could not be anything but thankful. My son was not sick; he was fine. Our lives were just a little harder than most people, nothing like the pain I was trying so hard not to look at in all these families.

Several years into this normal life of hospital checkups, I was asked to go visit a little boy that was an inpatient. They were from our home town, and he had cancer. I didn't hesitate to go visit him and his mom. He was having a very bad day from his chemotherapy. After I had visited them, I realized how far I had came and how much my normal had changed. I didn't worry any more about sickness; I never gave that a second thought. I just wanted to talk to this family and let them know other people cared and were praying for them. I also thought back to how I had such a hard time sitting in that original waiting room.

One Christmas we were walking into a store, and there were a group of people asking for donations to help mentally disabled people. As we walked in, Tyler asked me what they were taking money for. When I told him he asked me, "Am I mentally disabled?"

I said, "No, son, you are physically disabled." I heard the volunteers snicker at our conversation.

Remember, he was still very small for his age. I was carrying him because if he slipped on a slick sidewalk, he would break a leg. So this sounded like a very deep statement from such a small boy.

Seeing the Miracle

We prayed for my son to be healed since that first sonogram. When he was four years old, we went for a routine check up to the hospital that had become so familiar to us. We had the same x-rays taken, the same routine we had walked through hundreds of times before. The doctor came in and pulled his chair close in front of me. He was normally a very straight-faced, professional man. He looked at me with the biggest smile and said words that still ring in my ears today.

"I have no explanation, but the disease is gone." My wonderful, faithful son jumped up and raised his hand as if asking permission to speak.

"I do! God healed me," he said in a very matter-of-fact tone. As we left the exam room, my son said he wanted to stop in a play place on the way home and jump in a ball pit. He had said many times when God healed him, he was going to play in a ball pit. Me, being a woman of great faith (note: sarcasm) went back to the doctor and told him what my little boy wanted to do and ask if it was safe.

The doctor elaborated, "Judging from these x-rays, I see no reason he cannot do anything any *normal* child does now."

I didn't know how to let him be normal at first. I had guarded his every move for four years. This was going to take some time for me to let go. My son looked at me and said, "Mom, God doesn't heal half way." We did find a play place on the way home and for the first time in his life, he jumped in the balls. We went home and told his sister he was healed. The same wonderful, prayer-warrior sister that had been so insistent that his leg was healed when he was born, looked up at me and said, "That didn't take God very long. We have only been praying for him to be healed for four years." My little girl was only eight years old. She had prayed half of her life for her brother to be healed, but it hadn't taken God very long. How beautiful is the faith of a child—such a lesson to adults that are so impatient for prayers to be answered.

It was a church night for us. He and I were called to the front, and we shared our miracle. I still remember how loud the praises rang through the auditorium that night it made my ears ring.

Shortly after Tyler was healed, we headed to church on a very rainy Sunday morning. I pulled into the handicapped parking spot that I had used for years. My son's sweet little voice came from the back seat.

"Mom, I'm healed now. We don't need to park here anymore." We were the only family in the church that used these spots at that time, what was one more time? One more time would have belittled what God had done for us. I backed out, parked a million miles away, and we ran through the rain laughing all the way.

The first spring after his healing, my little boy was playing outside. He fell down and scraped his knee for the first time. He came in to me and pointed down at his bleeding knee. He had a confused look on his face and said, "What is this?"

I said, "Oh you scraped your knee, and it's bleeding."

He then replied in a totally disgusted tone, "This is not funny! This hurts!"

It is a whole different perspective when you didn't fall as a small child and learn these things. It was all I could do to keep from laughing as I bandaged his first skinned knee. It was a skinned knee, not a broken leg. He was turning into a normal little boy.

My son is a grown man now, and he stands five ten—not bad for a child that was never suppose to reach five feet! But as he said when he was young, God doesn't heal half way.

WHAT NORMAL LOOKS LIKE AFTER SHAKEN BABY SYNDROME

The early years were sometimes very intense. Just trying to figure out what Wesley knew and didn't know was difficult. When a child has no words and can't make eye contact with you, it is much harder to understand what he thinks or wants. We as humans depend so much on normal body language to communicate with each other. When that normal body language is hampered by physical disabilities, it takes a lot longer to get to know the person and what his needs and wants are.

In those early years, I put my boy in many different school/therapy situations, trying to get him the help he needed. He would have times of severe self-abuse. I had to start keeping a sort of log of his life to begin to understand what was triggering these self-abusive episodes. It could have been so many things triggering his fits. He seemed to be on a continuous behavior cycle. Wesley would go to school one day and seem fine. Suddenly on the second day he would be agitated after school and sleep very little that night, and on the third day he would go into screaming fits as soon as we got home from school. He would roll around on the floor beating himself with his fists and biting his hands and arm—this would continue most of the night. If I sent him to school a fourth day in a row, the self-abuse would escalate to the point he would feel with his hands for hard surfaces and try to slam his head against them. If I kept him home on that fourth day, he would calm down and start to appear to be returning to my sweet little boy. So of course then I would send him to school again, thinking he was better. I reached a point that I thought the fits might possibly be seizure related because of the intense shaking and flopping around he did. After consulting his neurologist several times, the doctor wanted to see him in one of his fits; he did not feel it could be seizure related because of the amount of time the fits were lasting. One afternoon, after he had been in school three days in row, the fits started, so I called one of his older sisters home from school so she could sit with him in the car and keep him from seriously hurting himself. We then headed to the city to that same children's hospital we use to spend so much time at. He was fairly calm in the car. When we got to the clinic, he went into full blown fit. We had also video taped a particularly bad day to show the doctor. The doctor examined him during the fit, saw him locate a hard surface and slam his head, and viewed the tape. He was still fairly confident it was behavior and not seizure activity but scheduled an EEG to make sure. We returned for the test the next week. Wesley had to be sleep deprived for the EEG, which was not that hard since he seldom slept at this point. He did perfect for the test, slept through the part they needed him to. As he was waking up, he went into full fit again, trying to hurt himself and throwing his body every direction. The doctor came in and explained that his seizure activity had really not changed since his last EEG and when he went into the fit, the seizure activity in his brain actually decreased. The fact that it decreased showed that he was in complete control and knew what he was doing. I was devastated. I needed an answer. I needed to be able to up his seizure meds and end the horror that we were living in. Me, the tough one, started crying right there in the exam room. I explained to the doctor that we had been doing this for three months. If it wasn't medical and just behavior, I had no idea what else to do. The doctor told me I needed to figure out what was causing the behavior. Sounds so simple, doesn't it? We drove home and as soon as we got in the house, he started in again. I was sitting in an overstuffed chair, restraining him and trying to calm him. This was how he and I were spending most of our time, day and night. This became our normal. He was only sleeping about two hours a night, and the moment he woke up I had to get him out of his bed to try to keep him from hurting himself. I was actually sleeping on his bedroom floor to be able to get to him fast enough. So that day, I was holding him, praying for wisdom. I started going over the logs in my head; I hadn't put the cycle together yet. Then it hit me, I looked down at my screaming, arching six-year-old son and ask him a question.

"Buddy listen to me, are all these fits because you can't handle school? Because if that's it, you need to stop the fit right now so I know that's what wrong, and I will never make you go back."

My precious son stopped crying, completely relaxed in my arms, and looked up at me and smiled. I just started crying as I realized it had been months since I had seen him smile. I yelled for one of the big kids to get me the phone and called the principal and explained what had just happened. I told her to set up whatever meetings she needed to for he wasn't coming back. Convincing school officials of this was not easy because he would maintain while at school and fall apart when he came home. When I put my son to sleep that night, he slept all night for the first time in three months. Those months were some of the hardest I have ever lived through. I thank God often that those horrible days of self-abuse are gone forever, and I pray for families that live in the cycle of self-abuse.

Our days now that Wesley is older are very structured; we do much the same things every day. Any change to my son's routine is very hard for him. I work full time, so I have to have someone take care of him while I am gone. We are very fortunate to have his big brother, Tyler, be his care giver. (Which took years of fighting "the system" to accomplish, but that's another story).

Just the Basics

Wesley sleeps in an enclosed bed for safety. Because he has trouble knowing where his body is in space, he would fall out of a regular bed. When he wakes up, he plays in his bed for a while. We listen for him to jump before we get him up. His jump is a self-stimulation motion he does while sitting on his knees. This jumping is another reason he needs the enclosed bed. He is a full-sized young man, jumping on a regular bed would not be safe. If he is not allowed to do this before getting out of bed, he will be somewhat self-abusive all day. This is just one of many stimming behaviors he does throughout his day for calming. After about twenty minutes of jumping, he will let us know he is ready to get up. Usually he will yell "uuu," his version of up, or "mour," his version of good morning. We unzip his bed and change his diaper. Yes, my seventeen-year-old son is still in diapers and always will be. Potty training is a fairly high-brain function. Something a person with the amount of brain damage he has will never be able to accomplish. He immediately finds his "bug." It is not just a toy to him. It is his calming mechanism that enables him to handle life. He always holds it the same way, at the same angle, and shakes it the same way as he walks around. Our entire family and church family knows this bug and its importance to him. We all have one in each of our cars so we never risk being anywhere without one. I order them from a local toy store by the case. He goes through about two dozen a year right now. At one point we figured we had bought over three hundred bugs. He also chews on them and that, along with repeated washing, is what wears them out. While he walks around the house, we begin fixing his breakfast. We assist him in sitting down on a chair and feed him. He receives his seizure meds with his meal. He knows he gets meds in his food and will roll his eyes or groan at the bite that has meds in it. Next is bath time. We hold his arms and assist him in getting in the tub then we wash his hair and bathe him. He loves water and sometimes does a lot of splashing and laughing. The sound of his laugh is wonderful. His voice has changed with puberty and his laugh is deep and full. He will sometimes stay in his bath until the water is cold.

At this point, my son may seem extremely disabled to you. He is, in many ways, but he is also totally normal in many ways. He understands everything. Just because a child can't speak doesn't mean they don't understand. He has a very dry sense of humor, loves sarcasm, and greatly enjoys messing with new people who are nervous around him. He will actually back people up against a wall without ever touching them just to see how far he can make them move, rather than just walking around them. Then he will smile slightly and walk away. Wesley uses assistive technology to talk to us. He has a very sophisticated piece of equipment that has given him a voice. His normal way to talk is to go to his device, use two large switches to scan his speech options and find what he wants to say on it. It's a fairly complicated system, but his ability to use two button scanning shows his intelligence.

Simple things like going to the store are anything but simple for us. We need to have as much of his normal with him as possible. His wheelchair gives him a safe place in the world; he feels the consistence and protection from the unknowns the world holds. He has to have his bug, a tippee cup, a snack, a maraca, and of course his communication device and the switches to activate it hooked to his wheelchair. We are always on guard for things that will send my son into a sensory melt down. I can hear noises like vacuum cleaners from clear across a store, because I know he is not going to be able to handle it and we have to get away fast. The wheelchair also makes a quick escape more possible than if a full-grown young man drops to the floor in a sensory meltdown.

Even at home, we are on guard for noises that will adversely affect him. We never let a microwave *ding* at our house. You can see all of us jump toward it to catch it and stop it before that bell. He cannot stand the sound of the microwave *ding*. So for us, it is very normal to always stop it just before the time runs out. He will groan when the furnace or air click on, and he likes to be acknowledged that we hear the noise and that we know he does not like it.

He must have his music playing at all times. This is not just something he likes. Music is much like his stimming;

it is calming to him and helps him be able to handle the world. We recently purchased a new assistive tech device that gives him a lot more ability to control his own music, and he loves it. Before this device, he had to go to his communication device, scan for the CD he wanted, and ask us to change it for him. Now he can do it himself. The new devise is set up with the same two-button scanning system as his main communication system.

What the Blind Boy Sees

My son sees light and dark, shapes and outlines, and colors. He will walk up to someone or something and lean in really close, then touch it with his hands to see if it is a person or a piece of furniture. His vision changes everyday. Some days he sees a lot more and can pick up a toy off the floor. Other days he will run smack into someone standing in front of him. That is one of the characteristics of cortical blindness. Some days the connections in the brain work better than other days. I can't even imagine how frustrating it is for him to see differently every day.

We went to the zoo one time. There was an exhibit that you had to walk through in the dark. The surface would slope and turn different directions. Every once in a while, light would come on, and you were suppose to look at the lighted area and read something or look at the animals. After we got out, I thought how similar that was to things I expect my son to do. I want him to walk on surfaces he can't see so they seem to change without warning. His sight comes and goes much like the lighted pictures. It made me appreciate my own sight and understand his reluctance to want to do things some days.

Even on his best days, his sight is not normal by any means. He has no depth perception and what vision he has is mostly peripheral. So when you ask him to look at something, he turns his head to the side. It appears he is avoiding you or ignoring when he is actually looking right at it.

We have a light box in his therapy room to do vision therapy with. A light box is a very bright light that we put different overlays on and work with him visually tracking as we move them across the light. The hope is that the more we get the pathways to the brain to connect, the more consistent his vision will be. It has apparently helped a lot through the years. When Wesley was young, he had very definite good and bad vision days. Since he was about ten years old, he has had many more consistently better vision days.

Therapy, Therapy, and More Therapy

My son works with some type of therapist many days throughout the week. He receives speech therapy, occupational therapy, and music therapy through our local school district. Due to the severity of his sensory issues, my son is still unable to maintain in any school setting we have available. He has been on home-bound education since he was six years old. His program is totally therapy based.

We are very fortunate to also have a private occupational therapist that works with him on a regular basis. Not to mention, a dear friend that is an occupation therapist that consults with us and has introduced us to listening therapy. This is a program that helps retrain his brain to interpret sensory stimulation. He wears a set of head phones that have a bone conductor on the top that directly reaches the brain. Since we started listening therapy, his communication improved and there was a marked decrease in self-abuse. His concentration also increased.

Music therapy is my son's favorite by far. Partially because it is music and that is his favorite thing in the world, but to a large degree because of the therapist himself. My son was five years old and we were at a local restaurant when a man bumped into his high chair. The man apologized repeatedly. I told my son, this man is walking with a white cane just like you are learning to do. The man turned and was so excited that my little boy was blind too; he took his harmonica out of his pocket and began playing it for him. My son was mesmerized. The man proceeded to pick him up and talk to him. There was an instant bond between these two. We had no idea what the man's name was or what he did. Several years later, the school district called and asked what I thought about having a blind music therapist. The first thing out of my mouth was fear that my son would hurt him. We were still working with many severe behaviors at that time like biting and head butting when he got frustrated. They said the man had assured them he could handle the boy, so I agreed to let him try. Much to my surprise when this new therapist walked into our house, it was the man from the restaurant. When I told him who we were, he instantly remembered and his wife said he had prayed for that little boy ever since that day. So, as I said, they have a bond that he has with no other therapist. My son follows commands better, uses his hands more, and vocalizes more in music therapy than at any other time. We also have the tremendous blessing of a blind person to explain things in a way that no sighted person ever could. The help he provides us goes far beyond just music therapy.

In the past, Wesley received aquatic therapy. This was an incredibly important treatment for my son. Water gives him a full-body sensory input that allows him to concentrate better and reduce his constant self-stim behaviors. He could walk in the water before he could walk on dry land. He is more verbal in the water; he will say words sometimes. Unfortunately for him, the hospital in town ended their pediatric therapy programs because they are not as profitable as rehabilitation therapy programs are. We need access to an indoor pool because Wesley's body temperature does not regulate properly, and his seizure medication make him overly sun sensitive.

Autism or Autistic Tendencies

Having autistic tendencies simply means my son has many of the behaviors and mannerisms that appear in autism kids. Whether he actually has autism or not is always highly debated. Some doctors say autism is not caused by a head injury, so he only has the tendencies. Other doctors say he has enough of the tendencies to have an autism diagnosis. The treatment is the same, so it really has little bearing in our lives. What is certain is that he does have the sensory issues; in fact, he has the most severe sensory issues most therapists have ever seen.

The first time I ever saw a child with autism was when I was in grade school. My mother and I were at a local department store. There was a little boy screaming and rolling around on the floor kicking. His older sister was standing beside him just watching him. She didn't seem terribly bothered by his horrendous fit.

My mother leaned over to her and suggested, "Maybe if you walked around the corner he would stop and follow you."

The girl very calmly stated, "Not him."

At that time, none of us had any idea what autism was but when I learned about it as an adult, I remember that incident, and I am confident that is what the little boy had. His sister had learned to wait patiently for his melt down to end and probably knew quite well if she intervened, things would just get worse. The next time I encountered autism was in that hospital in Chicago with Tyler when he had broke his leg at my parents' house. At that point, I still had no idea what autism was. In my wildest dreams I never imagined autism would be part of my normal.

Autism awareness has greatly increased in recent years. Most people now have some level of understanding of the condition and that is helping our children to be better accepted all the time.

A Sensory Diet

Wesley is also on a sensory diet, which is a schedule that provides him a sensory activity every thirty minutes all waking hours. We call these his inputs. He can pick what he needs on his communication device or if he doesn't pick we pick for him. Some of these activities include swings of several types, trampoline, ball pit, massagers, therapy ball, a walk, a giant bean bag, aroma therapy lotions, and musical instruments. His swings give him a vestibular and proprioceptive inputs. His net swing grips his entire body tightly as he swings. The forward-backward motion of swinging gives a stimulating effect, while side-to-side swinging gives a calming effect. He needs different types of stimulation at different times, depending on whether he is sensory seeking or sensory avoiding. My son loves his ball pit—it gives him a full-body sensory input much like swimming. I am always looking for ways to give him total body input. These activities calm him and help him be able to handle the world around him.

Not Speaking Doesn't Mean He Doesn't Understand

As he proved when he was six years old and school was too much for him, he has total understanding. We just had to find a way for him to have language.

Through the years, we have had many screenings for assistive tech. In order for Medicaid to pay for devices, we have to prove he has the cognitive ability to use a device for communication. My son never ceases to amaze the teams with his ability to understand them and respond using their devices. In one of his first screenings for a device, he even amazed me. The therapists screening him were having trouble with their device working. One of them was working on it while the other continued to talk to Wesley. She started explaining to him that their device wasn't working. She told him she just needed to know he understood cause and effect of using assistive tech. She asked him to touch the colored squares she named if he wanted a snack. She asked him to touch red, he did, touch yellow, he did, and touch green, he did, and she gave him a snack. I was shocked, I had no idea he knew his colors. After that screening, he received a six-button, direct touch device that he used for several years. When that device wore out, he had another screening. It was decided that he really was using memory more than sight, so he started using the scanning method to access a little deeper communication. He received a newer model of the same device. Wesley mastered that device in two years and was obviously frustrated because he wanted to communicate more. We scheduled another screening. He again amazed the new team. They tried him out on several different high-tech systems. He could use them all. He showed his sarcastic sense of humor to them too. Then they had to find a device that could use a scanning method for him. He was then tested for the two button scanning, which takes a very high cognitive ability. Wesley figured it out in less than ten minutes. He was given a loaner device to take home and his own device was ordered. We quickly found out that Medicaid will not pay for a new system in less than five years. It did not matter that he had shown his mastery of a high tech devise, that he had jumped through all the hoops and proved his need and ability to communicate; they refused to pay for it. Medicaid also informed us that they would only allow him the loner device for a certain number of weeks. So we had given my son a voice, and it was going to be taken away. The fight began then! I spent weeks fighting the system with no help, and his loaner device had to be returned. Wesley's self-abusive behaviors began to resurface. I was heartbroken to see this. I had watched him communicate so much deeper and then I watched him loose that and start slipping away from me again. I happened to run into the director of our local regional center at a community event. I explained what had happened, and he was able to get us immediate funding for Wesley's device. We had his own device in our hands in two weeks. My precious son had his voice back. He was a little reluctant to use it the first few days. I think he was afraid it was going to go away again.

Education

My son has been under home bound education since he was six years old. Our local school district has no program that can meet his needs. Wesley has a therapy-based IEP (Individualized Education Program). He has no academic goals. This is due to his problems communicating, coupled with his extreme sensory needs.

This obviously is not how it should be. There should be programs available to meet all children's educational needs. At this point, the programs are changing and evolving constantly for very young children with disabilities. Unfortunately for us, Wesley is the first generation of older children with multiple disabilities coming through the system. I take some peace in knowing my son and I have helped paved the way for other children to be better served.

Things He Loves

Church is one of the only places we go successfully. We attend a small church where my son is totally accepted. The first part of our service is music. Wesley walks freely around the sanctuary during the music. He understands everything and as long as he can walk around he can pay attention and be an active participant in our church family. There are certain people he somewhat socializes with. When Wesley wants a friend to acknowledge him, he walks up and stands very close to them. If they don't realize he is there or are otherwise occupied, he will stamp his foot or make a short growling sound. When they say hi to him, he walks off very pleased that he got what he wanted from them.

Even though he feels safe at church, I have to stay right with him. He will go out of any open door. He could very easily wander right out the front door and be in a dangerous parking lot.

Several years ago, Tyler had his high school graduation party in a church gym. I was talking to friends and watching Wesley from afar. At that point, he really wasn't walking out doors without holding one of our hands. All of the sudden he just followed someone straight out the door. I ran, in three-inch heels, across that gym and out the door to catch him in the parking lot. When I brought him back in, Avalon said, "I've never seen you run that fast, Mom!" She was laughing so hard. I told her, she should see what I could do in tennis shoes. Ever since that day, I have to keep Wesley in my sight if we are out in public places to ensure his safety.

Things He Hates

Wesley hates being talked down too. Some people have a very hard time understanding that just because you are feeding him and changes his diapers he is not a baby; he has normal intelligence. This is his normal; it's just what life is for him. It doesn't mean he is lacking understanding. He will tell you on his communication device, "Talk to me normal." He will let people know it when they talk down to him. He also does not like being known as a survivor of shaken baby syndrome any more. He prefers having it called a traumatic head injury. I think he feels this helps people realize he is not still a baby. He is indeed my young man.

The Future

I know Wesley's future is not going to be like most other young adults. His normal is hard and time consuming for his caregivers. Most mothers have similar dreams for their children. We want them to graduate from high school, go to college, get a great-paying job that they love, meet that special person, and start a family. My dreams for Wesley are to learn to communicate his needs more fully so he can be adequately taken care of, to learn to feed himself, maybe even dress himself.

But really, isn't the only real dream any of us have for our children is for them to be happy and healthy?

WHAT NORMAL LOOKS LIKE FOR A CHILD WITH HEARING IMPAIRMENT AND ADHD

I fought an ADHD diagnoses for several years after I adopted Avalon. I felt like it is a condition that is over diagnosed, and many children are over medicated when they carry the diagnosis. I did not want to medicate her just because she had high energy. Preschool-aged children that are hearing impaired often appear to be hyperactive because they are trying to make sure they aren't missing anything that is going on. She had a sign interpreter in preschool who told me most hearing-impaired children her age appear as active as she was. When Avalon was in kindergarten, I had transferred her from public school to the same private Christian school my older children had attended. The school told me they were having a lot of trouble with her in PE class. They said she did not pay attention to the teacher and was acting out, sometimes running around wildly. I went to school to observe my daughter in class. I went in a little before her class time and sat in the balcony so she couldn't see me. Her class lined up against the wall, and the teacher started giving directions as she walked around the gym setting up for the game they were going to play. In that line of about fifteen kindergarten children, one waved their arms over their head, one jumped, one turned in a circle, one tapped their foot, one clapped their hands, and so forth. My adorable daughter would turn her head frantically from side to side and look at every child if they moved at all and copy their actions. She had no idea what the teacher was saying because the teacher wasn't looking directly at her. So Avalon performed every movement she saw another child do, hoping she was doing what she should be. She appeared very hyperactive and out of control when in reality she was being a little deaf girl in a hearing world. Because of several incidents like that, I was sure that was all we were dealing with and that she did not have ADHD. I was confident she would level out as she matured and learned to communicate better. That did not happen for her, the older she got, the more out of control she became. Our pediatrician was very experienced working with children with ADHD. He had told me from the first time he examined her at age three he suspected she had ADHD. By age six, it had become very evident he was correct, and we began exploring treatments and medications to help my beautiful, wild girl maintain in the normal world. I had tried every kind of behavior modification I had ever heard of or could find a book about. However, nothing seems to work. Our doctor told us the medicine he wanted to try first would have an immediate difference if it was the right one for her. It was not a drug that would take weeks to get into her system. He said we should be able to see a difference in concentration the first day. He went on to explain that medication for ADHD would not change a child's behavior. He explained further that when the meds give a child the ability to concentrate better, they can also concentrate on the bad things they want to do better too. He said if you have a child that really likes taking things apart, they will be able to concentrate better and find a hundred new ways to accomplish this. He said one of the biggest misconceptions about true ADHD is that the meds will make them behave better; the meds are to help them concentrate better. Often times, the behaviors increase as concentration improves.

Medication made an instant difference for Avalon. At this point in her development she spoke in fragmented three- to four-word sentences. Although this was a significant developmental delay, it was not all that unusual for a child with the limited amount of hearing she had. Only twenty minutes after her first dose of medication, she came up to me and said, "I have been thinking and actually…" I don't even remember the rest of the sentence, I was amazed. Her communication delays were only partially from her hearing loss—it had been more because she could not concentrate enough to form the sentences.

The first and most important step in starting my daughter's day when she was young was to get her medication in and started working. It took about thirty minutes for her medication to take full effect in the mornings. Until that happened, there were very few tasks she could accomplish. Without meds, she still had trouble connecting her thoughts, or even speaking in full sentences. In all situations, she needed short, single commands repeated many times. Picture charts and schedules are sometimes helpful with younger children. She also needed breaks in between tasks to use energy. Much of the ADHD behaviors have lessened as she matures. She still needs the meds, but now it's just us who can see the difference. If she misses her meds now, she just seems a little scattered. This could still be a significant issue for school.

While the medication did wonders for her attention span and concentration, we were still dealing with some severe behaviors. She would go from a happy-go-lucky little girl one minute to being totally consumed with anger the next minute. I learned from research that the behavior she displayed are indeed signs of ADHD, but I felt like there had to be a better way to handle it than adding more drugs. I was at a loss as to how to help my precious little girl. She would destroy her toys and then feel so bad about what she had done she would sit and cry. Her emotional state was always on a rollercoaster. I had been studying a lot into diet and children with disabilities. Wesley was already on a gluten-free diet. I attended a conference on autism and heard so much about diet and kids on the spectrum. One local doctor/nutritionist said he considered ADHD a spectrum disorder. I began to look a lot deeper into the connection of diet on behavior. I went ahead and started gluten-free diet with Avalon too. I saw a difference in her anger after about two weeks. While she was doing better, she was still having very intense behavior swings daily. She was beginning to show self-abusive tendencies during her worst times. She would bend her fingers backwards until the knuckles turned purple, and she would pull out her own eyebrows and eyelashes. Years before, I had a friend whose daughter had started twisting her own hair out, and it had ended up being a food allergy. So out of complete desperation, I made a consultation appointment for food allergies. The doctor was so encouraging and was very confident we were looking at definite food allergies. He ordered blood work. It was a very expensive blood test that Medicaid refuses to pay for, but I was desperate enough to come up with the money and give it a go. Even the doctor was a little bit surprised at the amount of allergies she showed. My little girl showed severe reactions to turkey, trout, and yeast. She had moderate reactions to gluten, potato, and peanut. She had mild reactions to about ten other things. We started with two months of eliminating all the foods from all three categories. Within two weeks, all fits were gone! She was happy all the time, laughing, playing—my baby girl was back! One by one, we reintroduced all the foods on the third level with no reactions. Two different times I intentionally let her have something in the severe or moderate categories, just wanting to test that this was not just all in my imagination. Within about half an hour, she would start yelling about things that didn't even matter, just an irrational fit. I also discovered when she ate something she shouldn't, the fits would last for four days; it took that long for the food to get back out of her system. We all became very careful with her diet because nobody wanted to put her through that. We were having some episodes of four-day fits that we could not account to anything she had eaten. After much research, I discovered that vinegar is made with yeast, but yeast is not listed as an ingredient. So any kind of salad dressing, dips, and sauces have vinegar in them. So we have added vinegar to the list and all fits ended completely.

All we had then was the occasional accidental food intake. One afternoon I picked her up from school and as soon as she got in the car, she turned to the little boy we carpooled with and yelled, "Quit lookin' at me!" in a devilish voice. I immediately ask her what she had for lunch. She told me spaghetti and bread and that the regular cook was sick. One mess up by a sub cook put my daughter on a four-day cycle of fits. But at least now we knew what was causing it and that it would not last forever. Her strict diet was very hard when she was young. I fixed macaroni and cheese out of things she could eat so she didn't understand why she couldn't eat macaroni and cheese that other people cooked. She also went through a time when she would do anything she could to sneak foods she shouldn't have. It was so obvious when she had eaten something she shouldn't because the extreme behaviors came right back; but because it didn't make her feel sick, she couldn't understand. She would tell me there was nothing wrong with her, that I was just being really mean. Avalon now is incredible at managing her own diet. She knows how to read all labels better than most adults and does not chance it on foods she can't check out.

School

Although my daughter is now blessed to attend a school that understands what it means to educate children with disabilities, it was not always that way. We only made it through kindergarten and half of first grade at the Christian school. Avalon's disabilities were just too much for her to be able to keep up with her peers, so we transferred back to our local public school thinking they would be better equipped to meet her needs. When she attended our local school, she still had a lot of challenges. School can sometimes be very demanding for children with ADHD. Every child is different. There a few things that do seem to work or don't work with children with ADHD. The entire traditional-classroom situation is counterproductive to hyperactive children. When my daughter was in a traditional school, she would often be forced to sit for a long period of time in class. She then would begin to be disruptive. When actually she was fighting to try and stay with the program. Concentration failed because she needed to move, stretch, jump, have some kind of physical activity. Then because she didn't get her work done, she would be restricted from recess, which would have given her the physical activity she needed to re-engage and get the work done. My precious child became more and more depressed. She fell further and further off the academic scales of normal.

There needs to be a different consequence for children with ADHD than to restrict their only chance to use the energy (hyperactivity). If educators could be trained to see the first signs that a child with ADHD is losing concentration, they could give them a simple task like moving a piece of furniture or a stack of books. It may seem like stopping in the middle of an assignment and doing something totally off task is horribly distracting. But for a child with ADHD, it resets them so they can concentrate and continue with the assignment. Moving a heavy item releases endorphins that help them re-engage. Without stopping and doing an activity, you are trying to make the child continue on a road that they are truly not able to stay on. That is when behaviors escalate and the child tries many different ways to control the situation. Some will become the class clown to take the attention off the school work that they have lost the meaning of. Some will get extremely physically active or overly verbal, some even get violent. These behaviors are way more distracting to the class than it would have been, if, at the moment that child lost concentration. The educator would have casually asked the child to bring her that stack of books or take a note to the office.

My daughter's hyperactivity was less of a problem when the school would allow her to sign. That took a deeper level of concentration that allowed her to do better work and the physical movement of signing was helpful to her. Unfortunately for her, the local school could not understand this. It could have been such and easy fix. You have to know your child and make them known to the educators.

My daughter's normal way to talk is with her hands. She is now proficient in American sign language. I am not, but I'm working on it. In our local school, she was not allowed to use sign after fourth grade. The school said she has some hearing and is verbal, so she needed to learn to live in the hearing world and not the deaf world. That sounds fine and good except it overlooks the fact that sign is her natural language—anything else is foreign to her and makes learning much harder. She did maintain an IEP for special education under the guidelines of other health impairment. The IEP addressed her ADHD as the main disability that affected education. From fourth grade on, I watched her fall further behind each year. I believed the "professionals" who said my daughter had definite developmental delays and that her ADHD was severely affecting her education. Every year I would force the school to add a paragraph to her IEP stating that parental concerns were that her hearing impairment was being discounted in her education.

In the middle of her sixth grade year, it became apparent that school was not working for her. She had become extremely depressed. Through a series of events, I finally realized that I did know what was best for my child and the local school was not it. One night we were reading a book together when I received a call from the school about some problems. I was trying to discuss the problems with Avalon and figure out what was going on. All of the sudden she sat straight up and yelled at me.

"You don't understand, nobody ever talks to me!"

I had a flood of thoughts all at once: my precious daughter had never been invited to a friends house, never had a phone call from a friend, had never been to a sleepover, or had never ask to have a friend over. These were all items I had brought up at her IEP meeting a month before. The "professionals" had assured me that she was quite social at school and had friends, but it had just became very clear to me she was alone. I assured my baby girl I was going to make things better.

I had a friend who had moved to another state years before, but I remembered her son had transferred to the state school for the deaf in high school. This young man was also verbal, and I would have considered him to have even more hearing than Avalon. I immediately contacted my friend, I ask her why her son had chosen a school for the deaf and if he had lost more hearing after they had moved away. She said he had not lost any more hearing but he came to her and ask to transfer to the deaf school. She said he had told her he never fit in, in the hearing world, he never knew what was being said behind him, he never really felt like he knew what was going on because he could only hear part of anything. I felt like that was the exact same thing Avalon was trying to explain to me. I went online that night and found contact information for our state school for the deaf. The next day I talked to them. All they ask was her age and if she was deaf or hearing impaired. I sat and cried as the lady on the phone described every behavior I was seeing in my daughter perfectly. She had never even met my girl but knew exactly what she was going through as a hearing impaired sixth grader. Our local district was working with her every day for years and had no idea what she was going through, they had argued with me about it and said she was just fine socially but had severe developmental delays. I made an appointment that day to go tour the school the next week. Our first tour had to be canceled due to a blizzard. Avalon was very excited for the tour though.

When we toured the school, it was incredible! Everything about it was perfect except for one thing. The new school was four hours away. I was very worried that my baby would feel like I was abandoning her. From the moment we left the school after our tour, Avalon was determined she was going there. The kids lined up in the lunchroom to meet her. No one even talked to her at her current school, and these kids lined up to meet her. She was somewhat overwhelmed. They all signed completely, and even though she did not, she didn't care. This was her new school, and she was determined not to return to our local school. She got to see the dorms and loved them. We talked a lot over the next few days about her being so far away. She did not feel like I was abandoning her; instead, she felt like I had found a place she fit in. While it is horrible to send my girl so far away, it has been the best thing I ever did for her. Quite honestly, it is a lot harder on me than her. While we waited for all the paperwork to be completed for the transfer, I did not make her go back to our local school. She had found her new school, and there was absolutely no point in making her continue in a place she felt so left out.

In the seventh grade Avalon took second place in a speech contest. She talked about her brother who has autism. She stood before a gym full of her classmates and their families, some deaf and some hearing, and she signed the most beautiful speech I have ever heard. She told everyone how she admired her brother and that she wished everybody understood people with disabilities are normal people. I sat in that gym with tears running down my face as I watched my normal daughter talk in her normal language.

Doctor Offices

The doctor's office held a lot of the same obstacles as classrooms for young children with ADHD. We expect our children to sit quietly in the waiting room and then sit in the exam room and be able to sit and answer questions. Something as simple as sitting on a therapy ball in the exam room uses a lot of muscles to maintain balance, thus, enabling them to reset and maintain a better level of control and concentration. Very few doctors understand these simple ways to help our children cope. They seldom explore the effects of diet either. They just keep prescribing more drugs. A nutritionist can help find non-drug solutions to so many medical conditions.

Dorm Life

Avalon loves her dorm life. She is always busy, always with her friends—everything a girl her age should be doing—just in a little different way than we think of as normal.

Weekends at Home

Our weekends mean the world to me. I miss her so much. I know the deaf school is the best thing for her, but it is not normal to me to have my child so far away. I have little control over her life in comparison to most mothers of daughters her age. That bothers me, as you know by now I like to be in control. My older children tell me all I really am missing is breakfast. They tell me that when they were her age, I seldom saw them during the week either with ball games and church activities. It's just a different kind of normal. But it is what's best for her and her disabilities.

The Future

Avalon's future is limitless. She can be or do anything she wants. Her school team has high hopes for her; she will take college prep classes in high school. She already has a list of four or five colleges that she wants to explore. I know my daughter is going to do mighty things!

WHAT NORMAL LOOKS LIKE WITH A HIDDEN DISABILITY

Having a hidden disability is a very unusual life. When people look at you, they see normal. It doesn't show on the outside. There are no immediate needs seen. I have been told, "You can't be too dizzy. You look fine." Therefore, one of the main struggles is finding your normal between looking fine and feeling terrible. Sometimes I find myself dreaming for a life I don't have, or maybe just dreaming for the life I had before bilateral vestibulopathy changed everything. I want to be able to throw my son's wheelchair in the car myself and take him on a long walk around the park or beside the river. I want to do it myself. I don't want to think about how dizzy I am, or how far the car is just in case a sudden onset episode hits. Our town has free weekends at all our local museums periodically. My youngest daughter has never been to the museums with me. But walking that much and moving my head that much is not something I can do anymore. It makes me sad to think I can't share these things with her; I did it with the older kids when they

73

were in grade school. Sometimes I feel like this "thing" that has attached itself forever to me has taken all the fun out of my life. But at this point, taking my children out alone is no longer my normal. I have to accept that and move on. Some days accepting that is easier than other days.

When you live with a hidden disability you have to become transparent if you want to get the help you sometimes need. Many people could view this transparency as complaining until they listen long enough to hear the whole story. Because of that, I am very cautious who I reach out to. I don't want to be viewed as a complainer or a needy person. As you have already learned about me, I like to be in control and don't like to need anyone. Unfortunately, I now need help with many things, and I hate that.

What Caused My Condition

My condition was caused by a long series of treatments with antibiotics throughout my life, starting with being a premature baby in the era when doctors gave high power antibiotics to all preemies to ward off possible infections. Obviously, some of the drug treatments were totally necessary like when I ate the contaminated ice cream when I was pregnant with Tyler. The antibiotics were what it took to save my baby. Other times it was probably misdiagnosis such as repeated antibiotics for chronic ear infections when the only symptoms were fluid in the ears and the real cause was reflux. That should have been easily treated with diet change rather than repeating doses of increasingly stronger antibiotics. Here again, the doctors seldom look at diet to treat medical conditions; they just give more drugs. That being said, the past can't be changed and once again I find myself learning how to accept the fact that God doesn't make mistakes, and I am here for a reason.

Living with Constant Symptoms

Even though dizziness is my main issue, I am very reluctant to say I am dizzy because that does not begin to explain what I live with. With my disability, I can go from apparently fine to on the ground in a second with no warning. That makes it absolutely horrifying to go out in public. I am always dizzy—it never leaves. Even on a good day, normal activities are a chore. If my head is moving, I have difficulty focusing my eyes. Shopping is practically impossible and certainly not the entertainment it has always been for me. Reading a simple price label is very hard. Friends will start talking to me from a distance in a store, and I can't tell who they are because my eyes can only focus when I am standing perfectly still or when I'm sitting down. When I walk, I have to fix my eyes on a target and focus on that spot the whole time I am walking. I cannot visually scan or look around while I walk. In order to look around, I have to stop moving, plant both feet solid on the ground, and only then can I move my head or eyes. This is the daily dizziness I have every minute of every day. Then there are also the sudden onset attacks of vertigo. Those are much more intense and what take me to the ground instantly. Positional vertigo can be treated with a series of head move/exercises in many cases. Those exercises will end the vertigo episodes, but for me, that also sends me into a relapse of the bilateral vestibulopathy. A relapse usually sends me completely to bed for about four days, and my physical therapy has to start over at a beginning level. Bending over is always hard, it makes me spin. Lifting anything can send me into relapse too. When I walk on stairs, I have to hold a rail and can't have anything in my hand or it completely throws me off balance.

The Panic and the Pain

For someone who likes to be in control as much as I do, this is horrible. I am now prone to panic attacks just at the thought of going somewhere unfamiliar. Right now, I need to get new glasses; mine are super glued together. I have made appointments, but I end up canceling them. I don't know what it will do to have an eye exam, that's a lot of eye movement. I can't go with my children either. If it causes relapse, I wouldn't be able to take care of Wesley. I can't go alone. If I relapse, I wouldn't be able to drive myself home.

Constant pain is also a part of my condition. Doctors aren't really sure why. One doctor said it's like my brain forgot how the muscles are supposed to work. So the conclusion is, all the therapy to train the brain to take over the balance function for my destroyed vestibular system worked. But now my brain forgets how to make my muscles work. The pain is not always in the same place, and thank you Jesus it doesn't stay in more than one area at a time. It started in my shoulder and arm. It was the most intense pain I have ever had. I had nerve conduction tests, MRI, and X-rays. Everything came back normal, yet I could not move my arm. I had to change the kind of clothes I wore; I could not put shirts on over my head. Along with intense pain I loose mobility in the affected area. The shoulder pain lasted about six months, and the loss of mobility a little over a year. Now it's in my knees, extreme pain with loss of mobility.

Exhaustion, the Never-ending Exhaustion

The exhaustion can be totally overwhelming. The doctor told me that it takes so much energy and strength just to walk and maintain in normal activity that exhaustion is inevitable for me. I have always been a person that needs a lot of sleep, now I know part of that is because I have battled this condition most of my life. Even though I am completely exhausted, sleep does not come easy. It's hard to sleep when every movement makes you feel like you are spinning or even like you are falling out of bed. I have to sleep sitting up because lying flat makes everything spin. So a lot of times, when I fall asleep, I will naturally slide off the pillows, then that makes me spin and wakes me up.

I seldom schedule two activities in the same day because I simply do not have the strength to do more than one thing a day. When I work, it takes all I have. I don't have the energy to run to the store to pick up a few things, and I seldom run any errand before work. It's just too exhausting. Being the caregiver of a child with severe disabilities is also extremely exhausting. When you put the two together, some days feel like I barely have the strength to get out of bed.

Then there is the whole housework issue. Forget that, most days it just plain doesn't get done, and I am too tired to care.

Therapy

Every day I need to do balance therapy. This consists of different types of eye movement, head movement, and body movement. When I am in my worst times, I start with only eye movements. Then as I am able to do those I add head movements. When the head and eye movements are tolerable, I add standing while I do them, then walking. If I really start doing better, I progress to a balance disk, therapy ball, and standing and walking over mats and pillows to simulate uneven surfaces. The last step is to start lowering the light or adding flashing lights. I have also started doing the same listening therapy that Wesley does. It seems to help too. The listening therapy is one-hour sessions. I need to do an hour or more of the balance therapy every day just to keep functioning at the mediocre level I do now. When I go a few days without getting all the therapy in, my level of dizziness escalates and with that severe headaches increase and the exhaustion increases. Then I promise myself I will never skip therapy again. But the exhaustion takes over sometimes, and I literally do not have the strength to do the therapy. So I live in a vicious cycle of desperately needing to do my own therapy, needing to maintain Wesley's every thirty-minute sensory therapy, and being too tired to get off the sofa.

Know the Person

One thing I have learned through all this is to be much more aware of others with disabilities that don't show. I am not naturally a detail-minded person. You can change your hair color, and I probably won't notice. Sorry about that. But I do usually notice a person's demeanor. I want to truly know you, the whole person not just the color of your hair. Hopefully, that desire to know you will let me be conscious of your needs, and I will be able to reach out to others that have needs that are hidden. I don't ever want to be the one that says, "It can't be so bad, you look fine." Looks can be very deceiving with many disabilities.

The Future

Dreams have changed for me. At the time, this all started I was training to run a 5K race. I had never been an athletic person, but it was something I really wanted to do. I walked 5Ks often while pushing Wesley in his wheelchair. He and I really enjoyed that. I really wanted to run just once. That will never happen now. We can't even walk them anymore. It wasn't a huge dream, but it was something I wanted to do.

I don't think too much about what the future holds in this area of my life. It's too depressing. Until Jesus chooses to heal me, this will not change. I will continue to be dizzy and tired and in pain, and continue to find my new normal is this area.

FINDING TIME IN A NORMAL LIFE TO ADVOCATE

One might think advocating for services and equipment that would help those with disabilities would be easy to do. One would be very wrong! This is one of the most difficult part for me. You have to figure out what is needed. Find out if it is available in your area. See if your insurance covers it. Convince your insurance provider it is needed. Provide letters from doctors and therapist, explaining the need. When your insurance denies it, because they generally will deny the first request, either appeal and reapply or find another source for payment. Convince the new payee that it is needed. Prove to the new payee that your insurance will not pay. Get letters of need from physicians and therapists because the ones you got originally are considered outdated. This all has to be accomplished with little or no outside help. No agencies point you in the right direction. No organizations are helping you find equipment or services or funding sources. You just know you have a need, and you have to be determined to find a way to make things possible. I know that all sounds very vague and probably not all that difficult, but it is time-consuming and frustrating. This alone could be a full time job.

I have recently ended a two-year battle to get my son a new wheelchair. He received his first chair when he was six years old, over ten years ago. Most anyone could see that he had outgrown his chair. But no one wanted to help fund a new chair for him. All agencies/companies were very confident that they were not the responsible party to pay for his chair. No one disputed the need, just that they did not want to pay for it if any other agency or program would. I did win the battle, and Medicaid paid for his chair even though they refused it the first time. Just because you get a denial doesn't mean you should give up. You can never, never, never, stop fighting. It sometimes seems that insurance companies deny the first request just hoping we will give up, and they won't have to pay. My son dearly loves his new wheelchair and sits very tall and proud in it when we go out.

As we have already established, Wesley is non-verbal. He qualified for a communication device. He is a very intelligent young man, but because of the severity of his physical disabilities, it can be very hard to find devices he is able to use. The first major device he was matched to opened up a whole new world to him. Finally, he had a voice! He was able to request things he wanted and say a few pre-programmed sentences. The bigger battle was to get him a higher-tech device when he needed it sooner than insurance deemed necessary. It took a few weeks, and a lot of going around the system to higher up people. I did get our regional center to fund his new device. Then when it was being delivered, we missed the big brown delivery truck because we were changing a diaper. I called the office and told them we were there, and they had to bring our delivery back. It was a Friday evening, and I could not make my son wait another three days to have his voice back. When I explained what the delivery was, they called the driver and found out where she would be stopping for dinner, and I was allowed to meet her there and get the delivery. Sometimes it seems like nothing is easy and if you let your guard down for a moment, your kids will get shorted in some way.

From the time I got my youngest daughter, I advocated for our local school district to educate her as a deaf child first. They refused, stating her ADHD was more of a disability to her learning that her lack of hearing. The school argued that she had enough hearing to maintain in a hearing world and should not be treated as a deaf child. I argued that sign was her natural language; it was what she learned best with. I conceded this fight for several years. However, I was proven right when she was in sixth grade, and she transferred to our states school for the deaf. Never ever give up when you feel it is right for you child. Fight the fight, advocate for what is normal for them. Never let well-meaning "professionals" sway you when you know what your child needs. When we first visited the deaf school, I found out that every hard-of-hearing or deaf child has the right to a sign interpreter if that is what the family chooses. Our school had refused my child the right to communicate in her natural language, and because I didn't know her rights fully, I accepted there decision. I stopped researching, let my guard down, and my child suffered for it.

I wish I had the magic formula to help advocate correctly through the system. The best advice I have is to talk to everyone you know about the need you or you child has. You never know who will have an idea or a resource that will point you in the right direction.

SUPPORTING NORMAL FAMILIES WITH DISABILITIES

There are uncountable ways you can reach out and give support to families that live with disabilities. All you really need to do is pick something that you love and share it. If you love to cook, surprise a family and take a meal to them. Who wouldn't love to not cook one night? If a meal seems like too much or like you would be invading their privacy, just drop by with a snack. It doesn't need to be a big home-made thing that took hours, bring a store-bought anything. It's just letting us know you care, you notice, you are there. One time I wrote a little note on social media about wanting chocolate. A few minutes later someone knocked on my door and handed me a candy bar. That meant so much to me, someone had noticed, cared, and came into my world. Incidentally, it was my very favorite candy bar too, and she had no idea. God is good—he took care of the details—she just had to be willing to serve.

Both of my younger children have beautiful pieces of art on their bedroom walls that were custom made for them by local artist. What a blessing it is to display those pieces of art in our home. The fact that these fine artists reached out to our family is wonderful.

If you are a carpenter, I guarantee there is something that a family needs fixed; but because every minute is taken up with things you can't even imagine concerning disabilities, they haven't begun to get it fixed yet.

Drop a card in the mail telling us you are praying for us, always needed. Send an e-mail of encouragement or a quick text. Some days a little glimpse of the normal world would help so much.

As I explained in my oldest son's story, I could have used a little help with house work. Most moms of children with disabilities live on the edge of complete exhaustion. This is probably one of the things that is true with any disability. The normal things of life are always put on hold to take care of the normal things involved in living with a particular disability.

Just Be a Friend

When you live in the world of disabilities, you can be very lonely. I think this is especially true when you are the caregiver. If you have multiple children and one is disabled, you always feel like you are failing the typical child. It would be such a blessing to have someone just swing by and take that child to the park with them. Avalon was in a swim team when she was younger. Between Wesley and my own disabilities, I needed help getting her to practice and meets. I was lucky enough to have several friends that stepped up and helped us. Sometimes I sat home and cried because I wanted to be the one that was watching her swim, but at least she was able to get to her meets, and she had people that cared about her cheering her on. She needed to be able to be a normal child for at least a little while.

When I was first going through my own diagnosis and trying to maintain my normal life, I was fortunate enough to have a good friend realize how alone I was. She set up a weekly meeting at my house with herself and two other ladies from church. Whichever ladies could, would come each week. We laughed, talked, and ended each time praying for each other. Those short meetings meant the world to me. I could not get out. I wasn't even able to go to the grocery store for myself, and I still can't do that most of the time. Just knowing that one evening a week I would have a couple of hours to talk to friends was so helpful. We women are very social beings and when socialization is not possible, we can feel like there is something missing in our lives.

At this point for my family, we aren't able to attend church very often. My pastor and his wife come to my house about one night a month just to visit. We have a meal and talk about everything in the world. They are young and energetic, and I love having them tell me everything they are doing and planning. They are expecting their first baby very soon. I need to have some form of socialization. We all do. It can seem horrible to admit you need someone to visit you; but if no one has noticed your need, shout it from the roof tops and find a friend.

Ask Questions, Don't Judge

I don't mind people asking questions about our disabilities. I find that much friendlier than being stared at. Believe me. I know we don't look normal. When I take my family out, it can be total chaos. There is absolutely nothing wrong with asking if I need help. If my seventeen-year-old goes into an autistic melt down, I could sometimes use a hand to get him out, maybe someone simply holding doors open for us or helping me get my bags in the car. I have left whole carts of groceries and made a quick exit for my children or my own issues many times.

Of course, politely worded inquiries are always better than some of the condemning comments we have all endured. I had only had my son a few days when we attended the other children's science fair. A fellow foster parent walked straight up to me, looked at my son, who was screaming in complete overload, and stated, "I could *never* take a kid like that." To which I responded, "No, you couldn't." I then walked away with my son.

One time, when Wesley was very young, we were in a checkout line when he reached up and yanked my glasses off my face and broke them. I heard people in line behind me state, "You would think she could control him better than that." I turned and said, "You might think so, but apparently not." Their faces were priceless. Shortly after adopting Avalon, I had a coworker ask me how I could smile all the time when I had "kids like that." I responded, "I serve a Mighty God, and I look into my children's eyes. How can I not smile."

The thoughtless responses come from all areas too, even from the professionals that are supposed to be treating our children. Once when Wesley was sick, I had a doctor tell me, "Treating a kid like this is like veterinary medicine." Excuse me, just because my son is non-verbal does not mean he does not understand he was just called an animal. I had a doctor refuse to even touch him to examine him once. I asked, "Wouldn't it be easier to listen to his lungs if I took him out of his wheelchair for you?" The doctor told me there was no need and just prescribed medicine. These are just a very few of the incredibly thoughtless comments I have heard. Thankfully though, I have had many more times that people are genuinely interested and want to help me. I find over all, the rude comments are probably less than the positive, but the hurtful sometimes stick in our minds much longer.

So the next time you see a family struggling in public, think before you speak. Remember not all disabilities are apparent, and not all behavior is simply an undisciplined child.

Bottom Line

Many of these things I have suggested aren't a huge commitment that would totally disrupt your normal life, but they would mean so much to those of us that have no normal life some days. Follow your heart, do what you love, what you are good at, and reach out to someone that really needs it.

EPILOGUE

My life has not been what I expected when I was young. I never dreamed I would give birth to a child with a genetic disease, especially after two healthy babies. But he was handed to me, a blessing. Without him, I would have never taken that beautiful twenty-month-old baby boy as a foster child or never went looking for that beautiful three-year-old little deaf girl. I would have not thought I could handle a child with disabilities. Each of my five children are part of my destiny whether I birthed them or adopted them. They are what make up my normal life.

Normal is different for every family. Whether that be the people in your family, the size of your family, your culture, or the disabilities within your family. It doesn't matter what your normal is. It just matters that it's your life. God has given it to you, live it the way he intended you to live it. And don't be afraid to share your normal life with others.